HOMELESS SURVIVAL GUIDE

DYLON LAWRENCE

LuLu Press, Inc.
Morrisville, North Carolina

ISBN: 978-1-79473-251-3

Library of Congress Control Number: 2019918305

Front Cover by Dylon Lawrence
Book design by Dylon Lawrence

Printed by LuLu Press, Inc., in the United States of America

First Printing, 2019.

LuLu Press, Inc.
627 Davis Drive, Suite 300
Morrisville, North Carolina, 27560

Definition of Homeless:

"A person without a home."

What exactly is being homeless? What is a home? Is shelter a home? Is a structure a home? If you are renting a structure to stay in, are you homeless? If you have a thirty-year mortgage on a house, are you homeless? Do you own a house? Do you own some type of shelter? Do you own the land that your house sits upon? If you miss a payment, are you homeless

These are questions that flow through the minds of many people every day. Homelessness is a very complicated subject. But the reality is, homelessness is a mindset. For me, home is where the heart is. For me, a home can be a tent, camper, car, trailer, apartment, house, mansion, castle or anything that provides shelter. There is no right way nor wrong way to have a home.

Many people prefer to travel and not stay stationary within one place. Many people prefer to keep their earnings instead of paying rent, dues, mortgages, and taxes. I've created this book as a helpful guide for those who may find themselves amongst the path less traveled. This book contains many great hacks, hints, options, and ways to make the most out of everything.

So... You find your self "homeless".

Don't worry! It's not the end, it's just the beginning. As long as your still breathing, there is hope! Let's assume you have nothing. No shoes, no shirt, no food, no money, no car, no phone and no nothing that most people take for granted. Just some paperwork or an ID that proves who you are. What do you do? Where do you go?

Depending on your environment, will depend on your immediate needs. Water, food, shelter, clothing, and hygiene will be the most important goals of each day. Because now, you are not just homeless. You are looking at life through the lens of basic survival. A mentality of survival is the most important skill to have while you are "homeless". Anything and everything can be used to your advantage. Any and every option must be explored and thoroughly thought through.

First Goal: Find Some Clothing

Being almost naked and roaming the streets is never a good idea. For an immediate fix, scout out some garbage cans for some thrown away clothing. This is not a time to be picky. Size, color, smell and look are not a priority this moment. Neighborhood trash cans or large garbage units will sometimes have thrown away clothing.

Another good place to look is in and around stationary clothing donation boxes. Sometimes these boxes become overfilled and people will place clothing on the ground next to them. Other times animals may get in and carry out clothing from within these drop boxes.

If absolutely no clothing can be found, it's better to wear a thrown away bed sheet or even a trash bag. Fashion is the last thing to worry about if your survival depends on wearing anything that improves your chances of success.

Panhandling

Panhandling is one of the most common words associated with the homeless. Everybody who becomes homeless debates on whether standing somewhere with a sign and asking for charity is worth their time. Though panhandling is not for everyone.

Panhandling completely depends on your location. Some locations can bring in as much eight dollars an hour or more. While other locations may bring in eight dollars a week or less. Panhandling is completely a gamble. It can also be risky.

While most people are good-hearted charitable human beings. You must also expect a few cutthroat hate mongers. Those who hate you and everything you stand for. You can expect to be cussed at. Even get trash and drinks thrown at you. You must also expect some people calling the authorities on you and shutting down the entire operation. Though during desperate times, panhandling can be an option for food and currency.

Sometimes its better to ask for other things besides money!

In a homeless situation, it's never a good idea to only attempt to survive off the charity of others. Some people are just not giving. Some people just can't afford it. Some people simply just do not care.

You should always have other tactics and plans up your sleeve. You could go for many days without a single donation. You could go for many days without even receiving a smile from another person. Most people look upon the homeless as the leeches of society. Charity determines upon luck and good-hearted people. You should expect only one out of every one hundred people to be charitable and those are generous odds.

"Hey bro, do you have an extra cigarette?"

Even if you don't smoke, asking another smoker for an extra cigarette is always a smart move. A single cigarette can be sold or bartered for other items. A single cigarette has a street value of at least twenty-five cents.

When you have absolutely nothing, anything you can acquire is always a benefit. Cigarettes and lighters have a great barter value. In most prisons and jails cigarettes are the currency, not money.

Some people will gladly give you a few cigarettes just to have someone to talk to as they smoke. Designated smoking areas are the best places to hang out for this method. Outside of most restaurants, stores, businesses and parks will have some sort of designated smoking area. If you look around enough, you might even find a few lighters or cigarettes left behind. Even a collection of a half dozen smoked cigarettes hold some value.

Always check the change holes!

No matter where you are or where you're going, always check the change holes. Check the soda machines, candy machines, snack machines, laundry machines and all machines that have some sort of coin change return.

Most businesses will have some sort of machine that functions this way. Many people will simply forget about their change within the machine. Other people may drop coins underneath these machines and refuse to bend down and retrieve them. No matter the reason, these are perfect places to always check when you are out and about.

Many places like vehicle mechanic shops will provide these machines for the customers waiting on their vehicle to get fixed. These are gold mines for the homeless, and you should check these locations frequently. Especially when you have absolutely nothing, any coin is better than none.

Keep an eye out for the year of your change!

Not every quarter is made the same! 1964 was the last year that quarters were made with silver. Every quarter made in 1964 and before have the metal content of 90 percent silver and 10 percent copper.

This means that your 1964 quarter or older is worth more than just 25 cents. Depending on the current prices of silver, your quarter could fetch a few dollars. When you're homeless, turning a quarter into a few dollars is extraordinary. It's not a very big lottery win, but no the less it is a lottery.

Every quarter made during 1965 and later are mostly made from an alloy mixture of metals. Modern quarters are about 92 percent copper and 8 percent nickel.

Everything is of Value and Use!

When you have absolutely nothing, then everything is valuable. Always keep an eye out for valuable materials on your travels. Modern-day humans live in a throwaway culture. Some times what they throw away doesn't even make it to a trash can.

You can find many valuable items amongst the sidewalks and along the sides of roads. Lighters, cigarettes, pencils, pens, bags, cans, bottles and even money. As they say, one mans trash is a homeless man's treasure.

For the homeless, a thrown away soda bottle is now a container. Pencils and pens to write and draw. Lighters can be used to make campfires. Bags are now a means to carry items. Cans can be converted into small stoves to boil water. Anything and everything is useful. Anything and everything you acquire is more then what you started with.

Welcome to the Public Bathroom!

Public bathrooms are essential for the homeless. Popular fast-food restaurants usually have the best well-stocked bathrooms. Here you can find the simple commodities. Toilets, sinks, and a mirror.

Public bathrooms also usually have soap. Soap is important. You can use this soap to clean all of the containers, materials, and bottles that you've collected upon your journeys. You can also use this soap to take a mini shower within the bathroom. Soap has the basic effect of killing germs and bacteria. Collect some soap within a bottle and take it with you! After you've cleaned some containers, collect some water from the sink as well.

Toilet Paper and Paper Towels!

Most public bathrooms are usually stocked with toilet paper and paper towels. These items are overlooked by the average person. Toilet paper is always a great thing to have when you're homeless.

Toilet paper can be used as a temporary bandage, coffee filter, tinder, seed starter, and many other things. If you have enough toilet paper, you can use it as a pillow filling within a trash bag.

There are many uses for toilet paper and paper towels. It's never a bad decision to stock up on these items whenever you can. These items can also be sold or bartered. A full roll of toilet paper can be sold for at least 25 cents. A full roll of paper towels can also bring in at least 25 cents. The price of these items will obviously be determined by supply and demand. If you are able to collect a few rolls of toilet paper, then you can sell them together as a packaged deal.

Bathrooms Closed?

Sometimes a public bathroom is just not accessible. Hours of operation and holidays will affect access to public bathrooms. The next best option to find tap water is to look for something called a “spigot” or “spicket”.

Many industrial buildings and businesses will have some type of water spigot accessible from the outside. Many public parks and beaches will also have accessible water fountains or spigots. This is a good source to collect tap water.

It is important to stay hydrated, especially if you're homeless. An average human cannot exceed longer than seven days without consuming water, this is known as death by dehydration.

15

Shower Time

Staying clean is a very important part of survival when you are homeless. There are many creative ways to get a free shower depending on your location. Many public beaches and lakes will have nearby shower stations for use. These shower stations are usually outside, so take that into consideration.

Many campgrounds will also have public shower houses for use. These shower houses are usually left unlocked and unmonitored. Simply hike your way to the shower house and get your scrub on.

Many public pools will also have showers within their facility. Sometimes you may be able to jump into the pools of local hotels without being noticed. Also, public boat marinas will usually have pubic showers for use.

Many popular gyms have showers within their facilities. These gyms usually give out free trial passes for new customers thinking about joining their gym! Showering completely depends on your location and availability.

Caveman Bath

If you have simply no other option, then taking a caveman bath within a natural body of water can be a temporary fix. Large lakes or rivers would be ideal. The important thing is to clean the bacteria and germs off of your body.

An average human should not go longer than a few weeks without bathing or showering. Those who have poor hygiene will be prone to sickness and infection. To have a terrible infection while also being homeless is not an ideal situation.

By just applying soap and washing off your armpits and other sensitive areas of your body can be a nice temporary fix. If nothing is available, then just dipping your head into a large public fountain can help remove the grease and germs from your scalp.

There are many ways to obtain soap and water. These two ingredients are all you need to practice proper hygiene. Warm showers are not always an option for the homeless. You can expect a few routine quick and cold showers.

Napkins, Forks, Ketchup Packets...

Make sure whenever your inside of a fast-food restaurant to stock up on all the "freebies". These freebies include napkins, forks, knives, spoons, mustard packets, ketchup packets, salt packets, pepper packets, straws, lids, cups and anything else available.

All of these freebie items are valuable. Especially if you haven't had a decent meal in a long time, sucking down some ketchup packets will help fight off the effects of starvation. Nutrients are nutrients, though obviously, you cannot survive off of mustard and ketchup.

Salt and pepper also comes in handy when you are eating an undesirable meal. Salt and pepper can help make almost anything taste better. Not to mention napkins and cups have many survival uses. When you started with absolutely nothing, anything else you acquire can only improve your situation.

Best By Date:

Many grocery stores will donate their expired foods to food banks. Though not all grocery stores do this. Many grocery stores and supermarkets will throw out any food past their expiration or “best by” date.

These foods are not necessarily inedible, but they are pretty close. Most expired foods are thrown out in sealed containers. So you do not have to worry about getting other germs on them. You may get lucky enough to find some sealed food thrown out on the day of their expiration.

Obviously, do not eat anything that smells rancid. Do not eat anything that that has visible mold growing amongst it. This is a typical risk and reward situation. Many canned foods and noodles can still be edible on the day of their expiration.

Foraging

Always keep an eye out for foods naturally available. Many wild onions will grow in plain sight within grasses and weeds. Learn the differences between edible berries and plants within your environment.

Even during a pinch, dandelions are completely edible. Everything from the flower, all the way down to the roots. Dandelions contain Vitamin A and Vitamin C. Eat them raw or boil them in a soup.

Never eat anything that you do not know of. You never know when something might be poisonous. Depending on your location, it will depend upon the available foods in nature. When you're homeless in a rural environment, you might end up spending a lot of time walking along roads next to trees and forests. It's beneficial to always keep an eye out for anything available on your travels.

If you find a reliable source of food, keep a mental log of its location. You may be able to one day return! Also, save your seeds and replant them in other locations!

Unknown Survival Tools

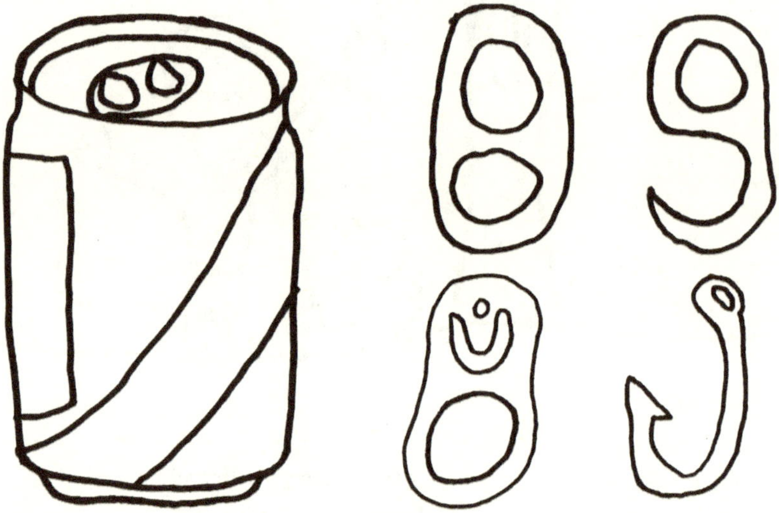

If you are unable to find food, then it might be possible to use the objects around you to go fishing. Simple things like the tops of aluminum cans can be converted into fishing hooks. Shoelaces, cordage or any type of string can be used as fishing lines.

Creativity and ingenuity is the key to survival as a homeless person. Converting items into useful tools takes practice. If you are unable to find food, then trapping and fishing may be the next best option. Everyday items thrown away into trash cans are perfect for repurposing them into survival tools. Use thrown away food for your bait!

Also, aluminum cans can be used as mini stoves. This is especially good if you are trying to purify water. Aluminum cans can also be converted into pretty sharp objects. Anything from nails to aluminum cans can be crafted into knives and shanks.

21
Hitchhiking

Eventually..... Walking everywhere will become tiresome. The average human can walk about 20 to 30 miles a day. This is relatively slow compared to a car or even a bicycle. You may find yourself in a position where only hitchhiking can get you to your next location. This is especially true if you are in very dangerous environments.

The success of hitchhiking depends greatly upon your appearance. The least threatening you appear will greatly increase your chance for success. There have been many horror movies made about murderous hitchhikers throughout the years and these movies are amongst the minds of every driver debating on picking you up.

Though, I personally do not recommend hitchhiking. The dangers of hitchhiking go both ways. You never know what kind of mentality a person has on the inside. Hitchhiking is a two way street of success and danger.

Exhaustion

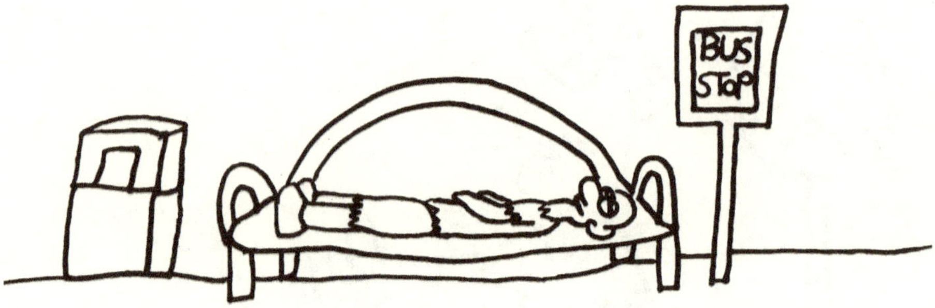

Benches everywhere seem to attract the tired homeless community. Whether at the bus stop or the park, benches seem to attract the homeless. Benches are great spots for temporary use.

I do not recommend permanently staying on one bench. Spectators will catch on pretty quickly. You can definitely expect harassment from civilians and law enforcement. If you only have the option of sleeping on benches, then definitely switch up your routine.

If you are staying within a certain radius of area for a long period of time, then switching up your routine is crucial. Humans are relatively comfortable with patterns and routines. This goes the same with homeless people.

Surviving as a homeless person depends on your ability to blend in with the rest of society. You should do everything you can to not appear homeless. This includes changing up you're sleeping locations and walking routes. The key is to not be noticed. Once you are noticed, a mental red flag will be placed upon you. If this happens, then you can expect a police officer to be waiting for you at you're sleeping locations and routes.

24/7 Lobby's

Sometimes the weather will prohibit you from sleeping outside on benches. Sleeping in the chairs of 24/7 facilities may be an option for you. Places like large supermarkets, laundry mats, malls, and even hotels are the most common locations.

Of course, this method also comes with great risk. This is only a temporary solution. Spectators will always observe your sleeping and contact security or the authorities. You should only expect to get a few hours of sleep amongst these locations. Though if you can find the right location away from the population, you might get unnoticed for a while.

Especially if you are lucky enough to find an empty commercial massage chair within a mall. These massage chairs usually takes a few dollars and will massage your back for a few minutes. It is not uncommon for people to use these massage chairs and close their eyes. If you find a row of public commercial massage chairs within a mall, then you might just get away with a good day's rest.

Homeless Campsite

Location is the root of success for a homeless campsite. This location should not be visible in any way. This location should be far away from the population. A campsite is usually made for a long term situation. It's even better to have multiple campsites readily available. Just in case one campsite becomes compromised.

Smoke from campsite fires can lead a trail directly towards your location. You should be very far away from society so that even a campfire is overlooked. If you must, you can just make fires during the sleeping hours of the night to help conceal your location. A campsite can bring a great deal of comfort to your situation. Tents and even primitive structures can do the trick. Use cardboard, paper, and bags for insulation.

It's important to not reveal your location to anyone else. Word spreads quick. You could be a target for theft and violence. It's not uncommon for the homeless to set up tent cities. This is a community of homeless people that live together. This could be a great option if you are worried about protection. This also means that more people may also bring more risk of exposure.

The Public Library

As a homeless person, you should eventually try to make your way towards a public library. Usually, each well-populated county, city or town will have a public library. They are commonly found near DMV's and courthouses. Even if you must travel a far distance to reach one, it will be time and energy well spent.

The public library will be your doorway to the modern world of survival. You will need some sort of identification to receive a library card. Library cards are usually free to obtain. Once you have a library card, you will have full access to the library's bathrooms, books, movies, printers, internet, and WiFi.

Locating a public library is a crucial process in obtaining knowledge and opportunities. Locate a public library by simply asking the local police, firefighters, and civilians. You may even be able to dial "0" on a public payphone to ask an operator. Also during emergencies, all pay-phones can dial out to "911".

The Search!

Once you have access to the internet you should begin to look up websites, locations, and organizations that can improve your situation. Search for your local food stamps office, homeless shelter, homeless charities, religious church charities, scrap yard and anything else that can be useful. Write down the name, address and phone numbers of all contacts for later use.

Also, check out the "free section" of commonly used buying and selling websites. Posts will be titled "Curb Alert". This means that someone has left some valuable items amongst the curb near the trash. These types of situations are usually first-come, first-serve. I've personally seen people giving away everything from TVs, chairs, clothes, bricks, metal, cars, and boats! The public library will often host little book clubs and other extracurricular activities throughout the year. Make sure to check these activities because they will often provide free snacks and refreshments!Mapping and Directions!

Mapping and Directions!

There are many websites and applications for directions and mapping. You can use these mapping services to get a good bird eyes view of your location. You may be able to even find a suitable campsite location by using these free services.

These mapping websites can pinpoint your exact location and tell you how far any other location is. Some can even tell you how long it would take for you to walk there!

Search up the directions of each location of interest. Write down the step by step directions on how to get there. This is a great and free way to get a good layout of the lands before you go about your journeys. The unknown is now known. Many free services and information can only be found on the internet. This is the way of modern society.

Food Stamps

Yes! If you are homeless, then most likely you will qualify for food stamps! Food Stamp services have different names throughout different states. Food Stamps is most commonly referred to as “SNAP” or “EBT”.

Food stamps services can sometimes be found within a Social Services facility. Food Stamp offices are required to set up ways to serve the homeless community. An address is not required obviously to receive these benefits. Though you will need to have some proof of identification. Exactly what kind of proof needed can vary from state to state. Those who are homeless and unemployed are usually the most qualified to receive Food Stamps.

Those who are qualified for Food Stamps can expect to receive a few hundred dollars a month for groceries. This is a guaranteed monthly allowance for you to buy groceries with. Acquiring Food Stamps should be a top priority for everyone who is homeless.

Religious Charity

Many religious institutions set up homeless charity programs throughout the world. Even if you are not religious or spiritual, these organizations can still be a good place to check out if you are homeless.

These religious institutions most commonly feed, clothe and house the homeless. You should be able to find out more information about these services through their specific online websites.

Not only can visiting a religious institution help improve your situation, but it is also a good place to network with other charitable people. Networking with other people is a crucial survival skill to improve. More opportunities will be available to you through networking. Though believing in some sort of spiritual strength can also help improve your survival mentality. If you are open to the experience, then this can be a very good option.

Non-Profit Organizations

There are many non-profit organizations that primarily focus on the homeless community. These organizations will differ compared to your location. A simple internet search of your area will expose these specific organizations.

These non-profit's usually feed, clothe and house the homeless community. They may also provide services such as job placement opportunities. Some will even give out items such as soap, shampoo, toothbrushes, tooth paste, toiletries, and other basic items.

Finding one of these non-profit's can greatly improve your survival situation. Most of the people working at these non-profit's are sincere and good-hearted. Some are volunteers and some are long term employees. It's always a good idea to be kind to these organizations. If you get banned from these locations, then you also lose their charity.

Homeless Shelter

Homeless shelters can be a good option for you if you need a quick place to stay. These locations usually provide showers, sinks, and toilets. Some places may also provide some sort of food. Though many homeless shelters are overcrowded with minimum resources to provide services.

This is not a long term option. Most shelters will only allow you to stay for a maximum of 30 days. If you exceed 30 days, then the staff may review your case for extension. Some homeless shelters will only allow you to stay for a maximum of 5 days. But when you do stay, you can usually get your Food Stamps card mailed to you there.

You can expect rigid hours of operation from these shelters. For example, you must be signed in by 5 pm to enter the shelter and you must leave the shelter by 4 am. They also usually do not allow pets. Many homeless people do not use these shelters from fear of contracting lice or bedbugs. Also, these shelters may force you to separate from your family. If you are a mother and have a 13-year-old son, then they may require your son to stay at a men's shelter.

Volunteer

Repay the favor! When you're homeless, sometimes its more beneficial to volunteer than to receive. Through volunteering, you can create very important contacts through networking. Many regular everyday people volunteer their time including doctors, lawyers, pastors and so on.

With large volunteer events, you can expect some freebies as well. Sometimes you may receive a new shirt for volunteering. They may reward your time with food and drinks amongst other things. When you volunteer, you also have access to supplies and other amenities.

If you volunteer for some type of construction project, you may even be allowed to take some leftover objects or tools with you. Volunteering is a great way to be apart of the community. You don't only donate your time, but you also have the option to receive as well. When your homeless, there is a tendency to stay isolated. Fear of judgment is hard for some. It may be psychologically beneficial to just be around other good-hearted people.

Selling Aluminum Cans!

Gathering and selling aluminum cans can be a great way to earn a few dollars. Many homeless people do this full time. Depending on the current price of aluminum will determine the paycheck you receive. Almost all scrap yards or recycling facilities will pay for your collection of aluminum cans.

This is not easy work, but you can earn from it. You should only expect to receive around 1 cent per can. This means around 100 aluminum cans is a quick buck!

Check out the parking lots of major sports coliseums right after a game! You may even be able to volunteer to clean the stadium benches after a local high school game! When you have absolutely nothing, a few cans and a few dollars is everything.

Check Out The Free Stuff Posted Online!

The free section is like not playing the lottery but still winning. Some people simply just have to much stuff and give things away. Many people would rather someone else have these items instead of just throwing them away. Many people would like to donate to organizations, but just don't have the time to do so.

No matter the reasons, this is good news if you are homeless. Stay up to date on the most recent posts within the "free section". These "curb alerts" are first come first serve. People literally just sit things outside for people to take. Use your internet access to write down the directions and location.

Anything from old phones, tv's, furniture, metal, tires, clothes, shoes, and hats can be posted amongst these websites. You can even find people posting free items on social media accounts. Make sure to investigate thoroughly, because some posts may be fake or scams. This is a gold mine for those who have absolutely nothing.

Sale The Free Items You've Obtained!

So you've acquired some free items! Time to sell and make some profit! Use the same websites and social media accounts to re-sale everything! Many things that cannot be sold, may possibly still be useful to trade. Try a pawn shop!

This method is basically all profit. When you started with nothing, anything you've sold is considered progress. If you can't sell a specific item, then scrapping it may also be profitable.

Let's say you've obtained a free broken fridge. Instead of selling a broken fridge, you can strip the fridge of its aluminum and copper. The items you've acquired may be worthless, but the material that makes up the item is valuable.

Try to look at all items as profitable. With networking, you may be able to sell your items through your contacts. If you happen to come across a football mug, then you may be able to sell it to one of your contacts that collect such items.

Large Apartment Building Dumpsters!

The dumpsters of apartment buildings are usually overlooked as a way of profit! When people move out of apartments, they will sometimes throw away their extra items. Also when people are evicted for whatever reasons, their belongings are usually left at the dumpsters. Some people simply buy new items and leave their old items at the dumpsters. Whatever the reason, these apartment building dumpsters are important to keep an eye on.

I've personally seen things like bed frames, mattresses, tables, chairs, fridges, and stoves just left beside of these dumpsters. For a homeless person that has nothing, this is also a potential gold mine. Many of these large items can be sold. Many of these items can be scrapped for their metal content.

Always keep tabs on these dumpsters. This is a game of chance, but the odds are in your favor.

Upgrade Your Situation!

Whenever you can, always improve your situation! Sometimes its more beneficial to keep certain items, then to sale them. A few cooking pots and clean containers are always a good idea to keep. No matter how you've obtained these items, always keep the best ones for yourself.

Upgrade to a tent! Sometimes it is psychologically beneficial to own some sort of shelter. Even if it's a small little cheap tent, it's absolutely better then nothing. Also if you have an easy portable tent, this means you will become more mobile. To me, a tent can be a home. For some people, a tent is all they need.

Depending on your situation will also depend on the items you need. Small portable items are important to acquire. You never know when you may have to get up and leave in a hurry. Anything you can do to improve your situation is a great survival skill.

Get A Good Knife!

Your chances of success during any survival situation is greatly increased by having a good knife in your possession. A knife is one of the most versatile multi-tools available. You should make it a habit to always keep one on your persons at all times. Of course, make sure it's the right size to legally carry in your state.

It's always better to have a knife, then not to have one. A knife has the ability to cut wood and other materials as need. Many knives can be used to open up canned foods. A knife can be essential when trying to create a campsite. A knife can also be used to skin and cut fresh fish. A knife can also be a deterrent to attackers that wish to do you harm. It's a sad fact that many homeless people across the country are victims of assault and murder every day. Help decrease your odds of bodily injury by carrying protection.

The Plastic Bag!

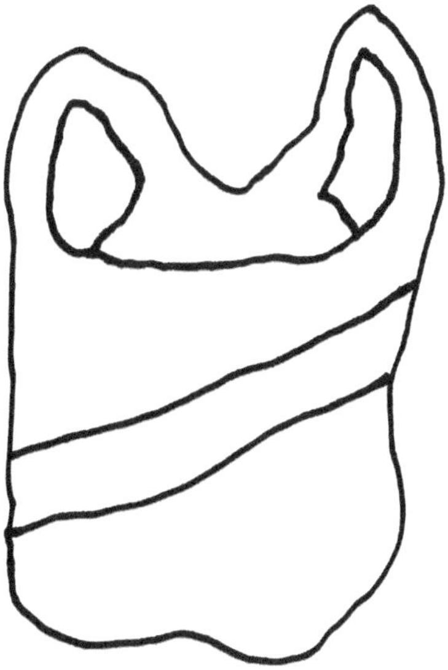

Never underestimate the value of a plastic bag! You can never have enough of them when you are homeless. They are light but also strong! They can be wrapped together to make rope and cordage! They also make great containers for carrying. They are also great for keeping your valuable items waterproof

Multiple plastic bags can also be used for insulation. Insulation for your tent, campsite, clothes or whatever else you may need. Plastic bags can also help create a barrier to protect yourself from rainfall. Fill a plastic bag with dirt and you have an instant sandbag! Wear them over your feet and hands to keep them dry! If you ever get lost in the wilderness, you can use plastic bags to mark the trails already traveled. Fill a bunch together and make a sleeping mat! Use plastic bags as a makeshift fishing net! There are so many uses for a plastic bag. They make a great survival tool for the homeless, especially because they are usually available anywhere and everywhere.

Obtain a Bicycle!

Everyone is more progressive when they have the ability to cover more ground during the day. The average human can walk about 20 to 30 miles a day. That same average human on a bicycle can travel about 40 to 60 miles a day. This is pretty significant for the homeless community. Instead of one or two stops a day, they may be able to squeeze in three or four stops a day.

This means more stops at the public library, scrap yard, and other miscellaneous locations. This also means that the opportunities to obtain money greatly increase. Nothing expensive is necessary. As long as you are able to move on it, then you are already on the right track.

Check out the “free section” online! You might get lucky and find someone who is giving one away near you!

Get Yourself a Mail Box!

Having a P.O. box can be very beneficial to a homeless person. Depending on your area will depend on the price to rent a mailbox. You can rent a mailbox from the national wide postal service or you can get one from other delivery companies. You can expect to pay anywhere from 6 to 25 dollars a month or more. If you can eventually afford it, you can pay for 6 months at a time. This ensures a somewhat stable system.

Many companies do not mail to P.O. Box addresses. Luckily, you have some options on how to write your mailbox address. For example, (789 Main St #33 vs. P.O. Box 33). Many insurance companies, tax services, and other government agencies will only accept a “real world” address. Some of these mailbox services will require you to already have a home address. During this situation, you might be able to use the address of a local homeless shelter. Once you obtain a mailbox, then essentially you have a real address.

Apply for a Free Government Phone!

Apply for a free phone! This is a free government benefit program. Those who are on Food Stamps, SNAP, EBT, SSI or Section 8 Federal Housing may be able to qualify for a free phone! There are approximately 15 million people across the US who have already done the same thing!

Search online and find out which company provides the phones within your state. Then simply apply online for your new free phone or you may be able to apply over a payphone. It's probably easier to apply online because they may require you to send some sort of proof of your certain benefits.

When you are approved, then sit back and wait for your new phone. They can send it to your P.O. Box address or maybe to the local homeless shelter. If your lucky, you may even get a smartphone with WiFi capabilities! If your homeless and receive Food Stamps, then you are most likely highly qualified to obtain a free government phone!

Charge and Access Your New Phone!

When your homeless, you have to find new and creative ways to charge your electronics. Many public libraries have wall outlets readily accessible for use. Get a book and sit down next to a wall outlet!

Basically, any public location with readily available wall outlets can be considered a good option. Fast food restaurants and coffee shops are good locations to wait and charge your electronics.

Now that you have a phone, you are accessible to the whole world! Buying and selling items just became easier. If you have WiFi capabilities, then you have even more access to the world! You may not have to rely upon the public library for internet access anymore. You now have every public location that offers free WiFi to do the same exact things.

Plan and map your journey on the go! Apply and access anything and everything!

Get a Bank Account!

Getting a bank account is somewhat important. Especially if you want to buy and sell items over the internet. Many online auction websites will require you to have a bank account before buying or selling anything.

The world is also becoming very paperless. As a homeless person, it's never a good idea to carry around your entire life savings of cash. This is an opportunity for disaster. Accidents happen all the time, it would be a shame if you lost all of your hard-earned cash due to a natural disaster. It is even worse if you get robbed of all of your life savings as you sleep.

For these reasons, it is important to keep your money safe. Some banks will allow the homeless community to open a checking account with absolutely no deposit. If you cannot gain a bank account, then purchasing a pre-paid debit card may be an option for you. These cards are similar to a regular debit card.

Thrift Shops and Yard Sales

Eventually, you will want to have at least one good professional outfit. It's basic nature for humans to judge people on appearance. Thrift shops and yard sales are great places to find deals on good clothes. I've personally bought an entire great looking suit from a thrift shop for 12 dollars.

When you have a good appearance, you are more likely to obtain the results you desire. Everything from making new friends to doing well at a job interview. You will also become more trustworthy. The outside appearance is a direct reflection of the inside of someone's mind.

Yard sales are often great places to find valuable items for a bargain price. You may even be able to barter with the yard sale owner. Since a yard sale is a private vendor, bartering is more accepted than other places. A good set of interview clothes could be the difference between employed or unemployed.

King of Survival!

Always improve your situation! We started with absolutely nothing, now we have water, food, shelter, clothing and hygiene solutions. Nothing is stopping you from achieving your goals!

You also have an ID, address, phone, and a bank account! These are the few things that most employers require. Check out the local staffing agency for job opportunities! You can even check the local newspaper or online ads.

From here you have many options. For many people, finding and obtaining a job is very difficult. Mental illness, drug addiction, and criminal records are the main reasons for long term unemployment. Divorce, alimony and child support are even more factors that play a role. To survive on the path less traveled takes great courage and heart. I hope this basic survival guide helps you amongst your journeys friend!

Notes:

Notes:

Notes:

Disclaimer:

The information provided within this book is only designed to provide helpful information to the subject disclosed. This book is not meant to be used, nor should it be used to diagnose or treat any medical condition.

The publisher and author are not responsible for any specific health needs or reliable for negative consequences of actions to any pension reading or regarding the information within this book.

All the information within this book is meant for entertainment and research purposes only and does not constitute endorsement by the publisher or author. The author and publisher are not responsible for any matter or content within this book. This book in no way encourages criminal behavior. Nothing in this book should be attempted or recreated. Laws are always changing. Therefore what was legal may now be illegal.

All of the material within this book is provided as informative literature only and may not be construed as medical advice or instruction. No action or inaction should be taken based solely on the contents of this book. Readers should instead seek appropriate health and mental professionals for consultation relating to their health or well being.

Readers are solely responsible for their actions. The information within this book is intended to be solely informational towards the reader. The information contained within this book is for educational purposes only.

This book is for informational and entertainment purposes only and is not a substitute for medical advice or treatment. Please consult a physician whenever you plan to make significant changes to your diet. If you have a medical problem always consult your physician first.

www.ingramcontent.com/pod-product-compliance
Lightning Source LLC
LaVergne TN
LVHW090854100726
842905LV00053B/248
* 9 7 8 1 7 9 4 7 3 2 5 1 3 *